Famous Regiments on Cigarette & Trade Cards

THE REGIMENTS OF WALES

THE WELSH GUARDS

THE ROYAL WELSH FUSILIERS

THE ROYAL REGIMENT OF WALES
(24th/41st)

THE MONMOUTHSHIRE REGIMENT

By
David J. Hunter

Produced & Published by
David J. Hunter
11 Sunnindale Drive
Tollerton
Nottingham NG12 4ES

First published 2000

British Regiments
Issued by the Army Careers Information Office 1991

Printed by
Adlard Print & Reprographics
Ruddington
Nottingham

ISBN 0 9533738 8 6

INTRODUCTION

The object of the books in the Famous Regiments Series is to illustrate the wide selection of both cigarette and trade cards that are available showing different regiments and Corps of the British Army. It must be borne in mind that the vast majority of these cards were issued after the amalgamations of 1881, but before those of recent years, such as 'Options for Change'. By their nature and size they were extremely suitable for showing individuals, such as Victoria Cross winners, leading generals and other prominent personalities. They also show the full dress of the period making them very attractive and collectable. Indeed cards issued at or before the Boer War can be, in some instances, very difficult to find and valuable, whereas those produced just before the Second World War are more readily available and less expensive.

The Cartophilic of Society of Great Britain, the name of the organisation for collectors of such cards and formed in 1938, has produced a number of reference books over the years, which are of invaluable assistance in identifying the numerous sets issued in just over a century of the hobby.

This particular book, the ninth in the series, is of the Regiments of Wales, namely The Welsh Guards, The Royal Welch Fusiliers, The Royal Regiment of Wales (24th/41st Foot) and The Monmouthshire Regiment. As well as illustrating the uniforms, badges and Regimental Colours of the three regiments, it also shows a number of Victoria Cross winners and other leading personalities who served them, including many of those who fought in the Zulu War.

The illustrations of cigarette cards issued by E. & W. Anstie, W.A. & A.C. Churchman, Franklyn Davey, Hignett Bros. & Co., Lambert & Butler, Stephen Mitchell & Son, Ogdens Ltd., John Player & Sons, F. & J. Smith and W.D. & H.O. Wills are reproduced with the kind permission of Imperial Tobacco Ltd.

The illustrations of cigarette cards of the British American Tobacco Company and Gallaher Ltd. are also reproduced with the kind permission of the two companies concerned.

The illustrations of the cards issued by the Victoria Gallery are reproduced with the kind permission of the artist Bob Marrion.

Whether a student of military history or a cigarette card collector, I hope that this book is of interest to all readers and certainly it shows how much useful and interesting information is contained on such cards.

David J. Hunter

HISTORY OF CIGARETTE CARDS

With the advent of cigarette wrapping machines in the late 19th Century plain pieces of card were used as 'stiffeners' for cigarette packets, bearing mind that these were flimsy paper packages unlike the card boxes of today. By the late 1870's the tobacco manufacturers in the USA. started embellishing these cards inserts with advertisements and pictures. Smokers soon started collecting these cards in order to obtain full sets of the different series and the hobby of Cartophily was born.

By the 1890's many of the larger British tobacco companies were also issuing similar cards. Like in the USA. they began with advertisements and soon progressed to various series of particular themes (e.g. beauties, soldiers, ships, Kings & Queens, etc.) The early cigarette cards were produced on thick board and of an exceptionally high quality of coloured lithographs, although when card packets were introduced in the 20th Century they became much thinner. The first company to introduce photographic cards on a large scale was Ogdens of Liverpool, initially with actresses, and later with generals and other prominent personalities of the Boer War, which was raging at the time in South Africa.

It was Ogdens which was to become the springboard for an American assault on the British tobacco market. It must be borne in mind that at the turn of the century there were dozens of cigarette manufacturers, whereas today there are only a few very large ones. In 1901 James 'Buck' Duke, President of the giant American Tobacco Company, bought Ogdens of Liverpool and set about a programme of price-cutting and bonus schemes with the purpose of swallowing up the British companies one by one. However thirteen of the largest UK. manufacturers, including W.D. & H.O. Wills of Bristol and John Player & Sons of Nottingham, pooled their resources to meet the challenge and formed the Imperial Tobacco Company. They then fought back and were so successful that they even opened a factory in the United States hitting Big Duke on his home territory. As a result a truce was made and the American Tobacco Company agreed to withdraw from the UK and Imperial Tobacco agreed to do the same in the USA. Ogdens was then sold to the Imperial Tobacco Company. In order to deal with the export business of both companies outside the USA and the UK, the British American Tobacco Company was formed, based in Britain, with the shares and Board of Directors controlled by both companies. However Big Duke ended up the loser as when American Anti-trust laws came into force, the American Tobacco Company was broken up, as is was deemed to be a monopoly. The British American Tobacco Company (B.A.T.) eventually became a huge concern with factories all over the world.

In the early 1900s there were around 150 different tobacco companies in the UK., each issuing cards, and by 1919 approx. 1800 sets had been issued. Each of the Imperial Tobacco Companies (e.g. Wills. Lambert & Butler, Players, Ogdens, etc.) issued their own series, although eventually they were all produced and printed by Mardons.

MILITARY CARDS

As with post cards, the Boer War stimulated a large interest in military subjects. Although W.D. & H.O. Wills had issued Soldiers & Sailors in 1894 and Soldiers of the World the following year, these cards were not just of British Regiments but from across the world. The first all British set of military uniforms was in 1898 when Gallaher Ltd., a firm based in Belfast, issued their Types of the British Army. It consisted of 100 subjects, including leading generals, mostly painted by Harry Payne, a well-known military artist who was also a corporal in the West Kent Yeomanry. It was unfortunate that not every regiment is illustrated, but nevertheless a superb set. Another example of early excellence was a set of 25 Types of Volunteer and Yeomanry issued in 1902 by W.H. & J. Woods Ltd., based in Preston. During the Boer War there were many sets produced of generals and other prominent personalities, and indeed many manufacturers used the same photographs. The Transvaal Series by W.D. & H.O. Wills is a good example of cards with the same photograph, but with different brands advertised on the back. They also have different captions on the front to illustrate changes in rank or the fact that they had been killed, (e.g. Baden-Powell as a Colonel, Major-General and Lieutenant-General). Not surprisingly Victoria Cross winners received much attention back home and between 1901 and 1904 James Taddy & Co. produced a superb series of 125 Victoria Cross Heroes which was issued in 5 sets of 20 and one of 25 cards. These were of excellent quality, some of which are now very rare.

Indeed James Taddy & Co., which was a small firm based in the east end of London, produced a very large number of high quality military sets from the Boer War to the start of the First World War. These included Medals & Ribbons, Boer War Leaders, Admirals & Generals and Territorial Regiments, etc., all of which are well sought after. W.D. & H.O. Wills also produced a number of military sets, although most of them were only issued overseas. One interesting set was Types of the British Army, a set of 50 uniforms of the British Army that it was issued throughout the Empire, but with different brands advertised on the backs of the cards depending on the country in which they were sold. In addition, as is shown later in the book, other manufacturers also issued it, making the collection of the different backs very interesting. Almost every military theme was covered by different sets, such as Medals, Regimental Standards & Colours, Uniforms, Badges, Buttons, Generals and Victoria Cross Winners, etc.

The start of the First World War brought about the issue of a number of patriotic sets, such as Britain's Defenders, which was issued throughout the Empire, and a set of 12 Recruiting Posters, both of which were issued by W.D. & H.O. Wills. Gallaher Ltd. issued their Great War Series in two sets of 100, and their well sought after series of 200 Victoria Cross Heroes, which was issued in eight sets of 25. W.D. & H.O. Wills also issued a set of 50 Military Motors in 1916, followed by Allied Army Leaders in 1917.

Although the war brought about the production of a number of sets, it also stopped the issue of one titled Waterloo. Indeed some had already been printed, but with the start of the war it was felt inappropriate to have a set of cards which could be seen as anti French at a time when they were now one of Britain's Allies. The set was then scrapped, although a few survived and are now extremely rare and valuable.

During the war a number of silks were issued in packets of cigarettes by some manufacturers, the leading one being Godfrey Phillips Ltd. Many of these were of a military theme, such as Crests & Badges of the British Army. It was a set of 108 and was also issued by other firms. However silk issues of Regimental Colours were particularly attractive with the silk background making them look very realistic. Regimental Colours by B. Morris & Sons Ltd. and a number of similar sets by Godfrey Phillips in different sizes, some of which are illustrated in this book, are particularly attractive.

With the end of the First World War there was an understandable lack of interest in military subjects and it was not until 1924 that John Player & Sons issued a set of 150 Army, Corps & Divisional Signs, followed by a similar set of 50 from B. Morris & Sons Ltd. They were an instant success as former soldiers could relate to their former Divisional or other Formation Signs. John Player & Sons also issued a set of 90 War Decorations & Medals in 1929, which not only had British medals, but ones from every country that fought on the allied side, including Japan. These were followed by many other sets, once again covering the full range of military topics, including another nice set from John Player & Sons titled Military Head-Dress. Although by the 1930s great care was taken in the accuracy of the detail, Godfrey Phillips made an error in their set of Soldiers of the King, when they showed the Welsh Guards with a goat mascot. The artist was clearly mixed up with the Welsh Regiment and the card was repainted.

However it was in the late 1930's with the possibly of another war, that there was a flood of military sets from the different manufacturers. In 1938 John Player & Sons, issued a set of Military Uniforms of the British Empire Overseas, followed by a set of Uniforms of the Territorial Army in 1939. Both sets were on thin card and had gummed backs in order that they could be stuck into specially produced albums. All of the major manufacturers issued at least one military set in this period, such Air Raid Precautions by W.D. & H.O. Wills, Modern Armaments by Louis Gerrard Ltd., Britain's Defences by Carreras Ltd., Life in the Services by the Ardath Tobacco Co. Ltd and Army Badges by Gallaher Ltd. It is interesting to note that Air Raid Precautions was the largest run of any cigarette card set and was also issued by many other Imperial Tobacco companies. By 1940 there was a shortage of paper and cigarette cards ceased to be issued.

After the Second World War a few of the smaller firms started producing cigarette cards, but neither of a military nature nor of the same quality as before. It should be noted that Mardons of Bristol, which was a firm of printers owned by Imperial Tobacco, producing the cards for their companies in the 1930's, was destroyed in an air raid during the war. They were a firm who took their work very seriously and who employed a team of artists who researched and specialised in different subjects, such as military uniforms.

However in the 1970's a number of sets had been produced by some of the Imperial Tobacco companies, one of which was Decorations & Medals by John Player & Sons, and in the same format as the set War Decorations & Medals issued in 1929. Although for number of marketing reasons none of these sets were ever issued, many 'leaked out' from the printers, some of which aren't took difficult to obtain. John Player & Sons started issuing sets of cards with some of their cigar brands in the late 1970's, one of which was History of the V.C., a set of 24. Unfortunately they have now ceased marketing the brands concerned. However at about the same time the Wills Castella band of cigars started issuing sets of cigar cards, and although there has only been one military set, it was a superb one titled Waterloo in 1995.

The Amalgamated Tobacco Corporation, makers of Mills filter tips, issued a few military sets between 1959 and 1961, such as Army Badges - Past & Present which includes a number of the Army Corps formed during the war illustrated (e.g. The Intelligence Corps). It also issued British Uniforms of the 19th Century, which consisted of 25 uniforms of infantry regiments, and which was also copied by a number of Trade firms, such as United Dairies.

TRADE

For practical purposes cigarette cards ceased to be issued shortly after the start of the Second World War. However, there was still a public demand for them, and as a result a number of Trade sets were produced, mainly from tea producers, although unfortunately few of them were of a military theme.

Before the WW2 a number of trade issues had been produced, such War Portraits by the Elite Picture House and V.C. Heroes by Alex Ferguson, which were mainly the same as those issued by the cigarette manufacturers, and therefore of the same high quality. However the Home & Colonial Stores produced a number of attractive military sets of their own in 1916 (e.g. War Heroes and two sets of War Pictures).

Unfortunately the quality of the post 1945 issues isn't as good, but they are still very collectable. A number of firms issued British Cavalry uniforms of the 19th Century and British Uniforms of the 19th Century, both sets of 25 cards. Tommy Gun Toys issued a set of 50 Medals in 1971, which is particularly interesting as it has some of the medals awarded in the Second World War. One of the best sets was the one titled British War Leaders, issued in 1949 by Joseph Lingford & Sons, makers of Baking Powder. It was of the pre-war quality and consisted of 36 subjects, including Army, Navy, Air Force and political leaders such as Montgomery, Alexander and Churchill. A number of these cards are illustrated later in the book.

In recent years a number of the harder to obtain cigarette cards sets have been reproduced, with military subjects in their full colour uniforms being particularly popular. Also the sets of the series of 125 Victoria Cross Heroes, that were issued by James Taddy & Co. are now available for collectors for a only few pounds.

HISTORY OF THE WELSH GUARDS

The Welsh Guards were formed on the 26th February 1915 by order of His Majesty King George V. Indeed, recruitment was so swift, with Welshmen transferring in from other regiments, that the 1st Battalion was able to mount Guard at Buckingham Palace three days later. There then followed a period of intensive training for the next six months, before the Battalion landed at Harve in France on the 18th August. It then became part of 3rd Guards Brigade, the Guards Division, and fought their first battle at Loos on the 27th September 1915. A 2nd (Reserve) Battalion was formed at Wellington Barracks in August 1915. It remained in the England, supplying drafts for the 1st Battalion, which continued to serve in Flanders and France for the rest of the First World War, ending up at the little village of Douzies, near Mauberge, in northern France. During the three years it won twenty Battle Honours. However, out of nearly 4,000 men who had served in it, the Battalion had also suffered over 2,600 casualties, of which 856 were killed. The 2nd (Reserve) Battalion was disbanded at the end of the war, while the 1st Battalion remained in Europe as part of the Army of Occupation, being stationed in Cologne until March 1919. The Prince of Wales was appointed Colonel on the 3rd June 1919.

Apart from a spell in Egypt from 1929-31, the 1st Battalion remained in the UK between the two wars. With the start of the Second World War in 1939, the 1st Battalion went to Flanders as part of the British Expeditionary Force, taking part in the early fighting and the subsequent withdrawal from Dunkirk. Meanwhile a new 2nd Battalion was formed in 1939 and contributed a company of men for the composite battalion of Irish and Welsh Guards, which briefly went to Holland in 1940. A 3rd Battalion was formed and fought in North Africa and Italy. Meanwhile the 1st and 2nd Battalions formed part of the Guards Armoured Division, the 1st Battalion as mechanised infantry and the 2nd Battalion as an Armoured Reconnaissance Battalion. They then took part in the 1944-45 Campaign in Northern Europe and were the first British troops to re-enter Brussels on the 3rd September 1944, after an advance of a hundred miles in a single day.

Shortly after the war, the 3rd Battalion was disbanded and the 2nd Battalion placed in suspended animation. The 1st Battalion was then stationed in various postings around the world, having seen active serve in Palestine, the Suez Canal, Aden, Cyprus and Northern Ireland. However, it will probably be remembered recently for the part it played in the Falklands Campaign in 1982. Here it suffered very heavy casualties when Argentinean aircraft struck the Sir Gallahad at Bluff Cove.

The Regiment has won two Victoria Crosses, both by soldiers of the 1st Battalion. The first was Sergeant Robert James Bye from Pontypridd, Glamorgan, who won his award in September 1917 for gallantry in attacking and destroying a number of German a blockhouses. The other was Lieutenant, The Hon. Christopher Furness, although he won his medal posthumously. During the fighting in 1940, near Arras in France, he engaged a superior enemy force, and after hand-to-and combat, forced them to withdraw

The first illustration is an example of the Queen's Colour of the 1st Battalion of the Welsh Guards. As the card was issued in 1930, it shows the arrangement of the Honours that applied at that time. The current Queen's Colour has twenty-one, ten from each of the first two world wars on either side of the golden Dragon, with the 'Falkland Islands 1982' below the Motto 'Cymru am Byth' (Wales for Ever). The card was originally issued by Wills in New Zealand in 1928 and later in the UK by John Player & Sons. The other example is of the Regimental Colour and was issued by Godfrey Phillips in silk. This represents the first one that was presented to the 1st Battalion, and being a single battalion Regiment at the time, it does not have its battalion number in the top left-hand corner. In the centre is the Company Badge of the 1st, or Prince of Wales Company. It is red with three silver lions passant, and each time the Battalion receives new Colours, the Company Badges are rotated in turn. However, it should have had an Imperial Crown, not a Queen Victorian one. The final card is of the Regimental button and issued by Stephen Mitchell.

Regimental Standards & Cap Badges
Issued by John Player & Sons 1930

Regimental Colours – Series 12 (Silk)
Issued by Godfrey Phillips
1918

Army Ribbons & Buttons
Issued by
Stephen Mitchell & Son
1916

On this page are a number of examples of photographic cards illustrating life in the Regiment between the wars. The first two are from the set of Homeland Events that was originally issued by W.D. & H.O. Wills in the UK in 1932. They both show Welsh Guardsmen performing ceremonial duties in London, the first in full dress, during the Cup Final. The other shows the first appearance of the Welsh Guards at the Palace, shortly after they were formed in 1915. As such they are dressed in Khaki. The other two cards were issued by the Ardath Tobacco Company in 1938. Two sets were produced, an adhesive one in the UK, and a non-adhesive one in New Zealand. The first card shows the arrangement of the buttons of the Welsh Guards, which is in groups of five, being the fifth Regiment of Guards. They have since ceased to wear the white webbing equipment whilst on official guard duty. The other card shows a typical army scene, with the soldiers taking their medicine in typical military fashion, during an epidemic of influenza.

Homeland Events
Issued by W.D. & H.O. Wills 1932

Life in the Services
Issued by the Ardath Tobacco Co. Ltd. 1938

The first illustration represents the Panel on the Guards Memorial, which is in London, facing Horseguards Parade. It was designed by Gilbert Ledward, F.R.B.S. The next card is an example from a modern set that was issued by Carreras Ltd. with their Craven Black Cat cigarettes in 1976. It represents a Bandsman of about 1925. Finally there are three examples of the badge of the Guards Division, in which the Welsh Guards served in both World Wars. It is known as 'The ever open eye' and has since remained in use, being worn on battledress.

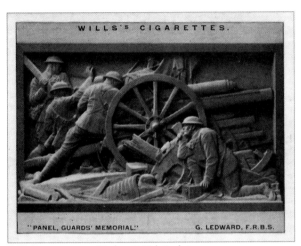

Modern British Sculpture
Issued by W.D. & H.O. Wills 1928

Military Uniforms
Issued by Carreras Ltd. 1976

Army, Corps & Divisional Signs
Issued by John Player & Sons
1924-25

Fascinating Hobbies
Issued by Beano Ltd. (Gum)
1950

Victory Signs Series
Issued by B, Morris & Sons Ltd.
1928

The first card is an example from the set of Interesting Customs & Traditions of the Navy, Army & Air Force, issued by Lambert & Butler, a branch of Imperial Tobacco Ltd. It shows officers and men of the Regiment being presented with leeks, the national emblem of Wales, and regimental badge, to commemorate St. David's Day; a tradition that is followed every year. The next card shows the tie of the Brigade of Guards, and on the bottom row is an interesting pair of cards, one of which shows a drummer with what appears to be the Regimental Mascot. However, the Welsh Guards have never had such a mascot, and it is apparent that the artist was confused with one of the other Welsh regiments. Godfrey Phillips quickly realised their mistake and re-issued the card with the goat painted out. Although it appears to be white-blue-white, the colour of the plume on the side of the bearskin should be white-green-white.

Well Known Ties – A Series
Issued by W.A. & A.C. Churchman 1934

Interesting Customs & Traditions
Of the Navy, Army & Air Force
Issued by Lambert & Butler 1939

Soldiers of the King
Issued by Godfrey Phillips Ltd.
1939

Officers Full Dress
Issued by UK Tob Co. Ltd.
1936

As previously stated, HRH Edward, Duke of Windsor, KG, KT, KP, GCB, GCSI, GCMG, GCIE, GCVO, GBE, ISO, MC, was appointed Colonel of the Welsh Guards in 1919, an appointed he held until he became King in 1937. As such there are a number of examples of him in different sets of cards, many of which are shown on the next two pages. The first shows him at a ceremony in Brussels with Earl Haig. The second is interesting in that it was issued by Bridgewater, a biscuit manufacturer. The other three examples show him as a Colonel, wearing different uniforms of the Regiment.

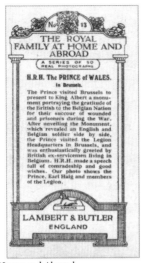

The Royal Family at Home and Abroad
Issued by Lambert & Butler (Overseas) 1927

Coronation Series
Issued by
C. T. Bridgewater
1937

Silver Jubilee
Issued by Ardath Tob Co. 1935

The Reign of HM King George V
Issued by W.D. & H.O. Wills 1935

Further examples of cards illustrating the Prince of Wales are shown, most of which are from the 1924 set of The Prince of Wales Empire Tour. It consisted of 25 subjects, some of which show in the uniform of the Welsh Guards, and was issued by Hignett Bros., a branch of Imperial Tobacco based in Liverpool, later taken over by Ogdens. The other card is from the set Our Empire Series, issued by R. & J. Hill Ltd in 1929

Our Empire Series
Issued by R. & J. Hill Ltd. 1929

The Prince of Wales Empire Tour
Issued by Hignett Bros & Co.

The Prince of Wales Empire Tour
Issued by Hignett Bors & Co. 1924

On this page are a number of examples of modern trade issues. The set Soldiers of the World was originally issued in 1966 by Barratt & Co. Ltd., a confectionery firm, and later in 1969 by Wiko in Germany. Dandy Gum, another confectionery firm, issued a set of playing cards in 1958 titled Our Modern Army, and although the quality and accuracy is not as good as the earlier cigarette cards, they are still very collectable. Indeed there are a number of errors in the paintings, too many to list. The large card is from one of two sets of Caricatures of the British Army that was painted by Bob Marrion, the well-known military artist, who carefully researches his subjects to ensure total accuracy. The set was issued by Victoria Galley

Our Modern Army
Issued by Dandy Gum 1958

Soldiers of the World
Issued by Barratt & Co. 1966

Caricatures of the British Army
Issued by Victoria Gallery 1994

Our Modern Army
Issued by Dandy Gum 1958

THE ROYAL WELCH FUSILIERS

Illustrated below are a number of examples of the uniform of the Regiment, the oldest of the Welsh regiments, which was worn at different periods in their history, including two of 1689, the year when it was raised. As can be seen they were dressed in blue at that time, instead of the red uniform that is normally associated with the British Army.

Past & Present – The Army
Issued by Teofani & Co. Ltd.
1938

History of Army Uniforms
Issued by Carreras Ltd.
1937

Traditions of the Army & Navy
Issued by Salmon & Guckstein
1937

Types of the British Army
Issued by Gallaher Ltd.
1897-98

HISTORY OF THE ROYAL WELCH FUSILIERS

The Regiment was raised on the 16th March 1689 by Lord Herbert, who then handed it over to his cousin Charles Herbert. It first saw action in Ireland at the battle of the Boyne and later took part in the victory at Aughrim, although Colonel Herbert was captured and murdered. In 1694 the Regiment landed in Europe and fought in the War of Spanish Succession, gaining its first Battle Honour at the siege of Namur. In 1701 John Churchill, later the Duke of Marlborough, was given command of the Regiment and the following year it was made a regiment of fusiliers. It fought in all of Marlborough's major battles from 1702 until 1713, including Blenheim, Ramillies, Oudenarde and Malplaquet. In 1712, as a reward for its distinguished service, the regiment was re-titled The Royal Regiment of Fuzileers, later Fusiliers. With its association with the Prince of Wales in 1714, it was authorised to bear three of his badges, The Red Dragon, The Rising Sun and the Prince of Wales's Feathers. When Britain became involved in the War of Austrian Succession in 1742, the Regiment went to Holland and fought in the battle of Dettingen, although its Colonel, Newsham Peers, was killed in the fighting. It also took part in the battle of Fontenoy in 1745 where it suffered over 300 casualties.

It was again in action during the Seven Years' War, suffering 40% casualties at Minden in 1758, where together with five other regiments, it attacked and defeated a force of French cavalry. Also, with the start of the war in 1756, it raised a second battalion, which, in 1758, became the 68th Regiment of Foot, later The Durham Light Infantry. With the start of the American War of Independence in 1773 the Regiment sailed for America and distinguished itself at Bunker Hill and Guildford Court, although it suffered heavy casualties at Bunker Hill. After the surrender of the Army at Yorktown the Regiment returned to England. During the French Revolutionary and Napoleonic Wars it initially took part in a number of small expeditions, including Santa Domingo, Ostend, Holland and Spain. However, in 1801 it took part in Sir Ralph Abercromby's expedition to Egypt and won the right to bear the badge of the Sphinx together with the Battle Honour of Egypt. In 1804 a second battalion was again raised and formed part of Sir John Moore's army in Portugal and its subsequent retreat to Corunna. It then returned to England and shortly afterwards took part in the failed expedition to capture the Dutch Fleet at Antwerp. However active service had seriously reduced the strength of the battalion and it remained in the UK. In 1810 the 1st Battalion went to Portugal and fought in many of the battles as part of Sir Arthur Wellesley's Army in the Peninsula, gaining another eight Battle Honours. Although its 2nd Battalion had been disbanded in 1814, the Regiment was again in action at Waterloo in 1815.

ROYAL WELCH FUSILIERS

Past & Present – The Army
Issued by Teofani & Co. Ltd.
1938

British Regiments
Issued by
The Army Careers Information Office
1991

The Regiment then became part of the Army of Occupation in France until 1818, before spending the next five years in Ireland. It then spent thirty years in various postings, such as Gibraltar, Portugal, England. Ireland, Canada and the West Indies. During the Crimean War they were one of the first regiments to land and fought at Alma, Inkerman and Sevastopol, winning four Victoria Crosses. One of the winners, Sergeant O'Connor, was commissioned in the field. After returning to England, they were then sent to China, but were diverted to India as a result of the mutiny. They took part in the relief of Lucknow. During the evacuation Lieutenant Hackett and a 17-year-old Band Boy, George Monger, rescued a seriously wounded corporal, for which they were both awarded the Victoria Cross. In 1858 the regiment took part in the recapture of Lucknow and remained in India until 1869. A new 2nd Battalion was formed in 1858 and took part in the Ashanti Expedition of 1873-74. Both battalions then fought in the various colonial wars that took part in the Empire. With the start of the Boer War in 1899 the 1st Battalion was posted to South Africa and saw action at Horse Show Hill, where the Commanding Officer was killed, and the Relief of Ladysmith. Meanwhile the 2nd Battalion took part in the Boxer Rebellion in China in 1900. Indeed it is the only British infantry regiment to bear the Battle Honour "Pekin 1900".

With the start of the First World War, the regular battalions were supplemented with additional territorial and service ones making a total of 42. It is impossible to detail the war record of such a large number of battalions, except to say that the 2nd Battalion, recently returned from India, was the first to see action. This was at Mons in August 1914. However, the 1st Battalion who went into action on the 19th October with 1150 officers and men, had only a strength of 90 by the 31st October. Ten of the battalions took part in the Somme offensive in 1916, five of them at Mametz Wood, in which four of the five Commanding Officers were killed. Together the battalions won 88 Battle Honours and a further eight Victoria Crosses, but also sustained almost 10,000 casualties. After the war the Regiment was reduced to its two regular battalions, which then served in various postings, including the North West Frontier of India. With the start of the Second World War the 1st Battalion served in NW Europe and the subsequent retreat to Dunkirk. Both regular battalions then spent most of the war serving in Burma. Meanwhile three of the territorial battalions landed at Normandy and fought their way across Northern Europe, while the 10th Battalions served in Italy and Greece. In 1948 the 2nd Battalion was disbanded, only to be reformed in 1952 and sent to Malaya. At the end of its tour it was again disbanded.

Further examples of cards illustrating the uniforms of the Regiment are shown, the first two of which shows the Flash of five black ribbons. They are a link with the days when soldiers wore pigtails. These were powdered and greased, and in order to protect the red coatees, the pigtail was enclosed in what was known as a "queue bag". When the "queue" was abolished in 1808, the Regiment was serving overseas in Nova Scotia, and as communications in those days were slow, it is probable that they were the last to wear it. When they finally dispensed with the queue, the ribbons with which it was secured were retained and, coining an old slang word for a wig, these were known as the "Flash". The example from the set of Uniforms of the Territorial Army shows a pioneer of the 5th Battalion in 1908. Just before World War II it was re-designated 60th (Royal Welch Fusiliers) Anti-Tank Regiment Royal Artillery, thereby ceasing to be an infantry unit.

The Reason Why
Issued by Gallaher Ltd. 1924

The Great War – Second series
Issued by Gallaher Ltd. 1915

Uniforms of the Territorial Army
Issued by John Player & Sons
1939

Cap Badges of Territorial Regts.
Issued by Walters Palm Toffee
1938

Eminent British Regiments
Issued by Cope Bros. & Co.
1908

Five examples of cigarette cards featuring regimental badges are shown, three of which are in silk. The first two are from the very popular set of Crests & Badges of the British Army, which was issued by a number of different manufacturers and in a variety of sizes. The first was by the British American Tobacco Company and is the only issue that names the title of the set. There were 108 subjects in the set, although in the smaller size there were 110. Both sets were paper backed. The other was issued by Godfrey Phillips as a set of 108, also in various sizes. Below are two cards from a set by Ogdens consisting of 192 cards and with many varieties. Finally is an example from a set of 86 badges by Anstie. Although this particular one is easy to obtain, some of the others are rare and very difficult to obtain.

Crests & Badges of the British Army
Issued by British American Tobacco Co.
1915

Crests & Badges of the British Army
Issued by Godfrey Phillips Ltd.
1914

Army Crests & Mottoes
Issued by Ogdens Ltd. 1902

Regimental Badges (Silk)
Issued by E. & W. Anstie
1915

Army Crests & Mottoes
Issued by Ogdens Ltd. 1902

On this page are a number of examples of Trade issues, although they are not all entirely accurate. The examples by Home & Colonial Stores and Blakey's Boot Protectors were produced during the First World War and show the full dress of the period. The set of 50 Military Uniforms was issued with packets of bubble gum and shows an officer of the Regiment in 1790. Glengettie Tea produced an attractive set of 25 cards including this one of an officer at Waterloo. The illustration from the set of British Uniforms of the 19th Century by Mills Filter Tips shows a soldier in 1849. The set was also issued by a number of other firms.

Military Uniforms
Issued by Chix Confectionery Co. Ltd.
1970

War Series
Issued by Blakey's Boot Protectors
1916

The British Army 1815
Issued by Glengettie Tea
1976

War Series (Different)
Issued by Home & Colonial
Stores 1916

British Uniforms of the 19th C.
Issued by Mills filter Tips
1957

The Second person of The Royal Welsh Fusiliers to win the Victoria Cross during the First World War was CSM Frederick Barter of the 1st battalion. The first was Lieutenant-Colonel C.H.M. Doughty-Wylie at Gallipoli. CSM Barter was born in Cardiff in January 1891, and after working for the Great Western Railway, enlisted into the Regiment on December 1908. On completion of his term of service he was transferred to the Special Reserve and was working for the Cardiff Gas Light & Coke Company when the war broke out in 1914. He was immediately mobilised with the 1st Battalion, which went to France in October, only to be seriously reduced in strength due to exceptionally heavy casualties. He won his award on the 16th May 1915 at Festubert in France. When in the first line of the German trenches, Company Sergeant-Major Barter called for volunteers to enable him to extend the line, and with the eight men who responded, he attacked the German position with bombs, capturing three German officers, 102 men and 500 yards of their trenches. He subsequently found and cut eleven of the enemy's mine leads situated about 20 yards apart. He was presented with his medal by the King at Buckingham Palace in July 1915. He was later commissioned and won the Military Cross in Palestine. He received a permanent commission with the Indian Army in 1918 and retired from the Army in 1922 with the rank of Captain. During WW2 he was a Major in command of a company of the Middlesex Home Guard. He died in 1953 and his medals are held by the Regimental Museum.

V.C. Heroes
Issued by Thompson & Porteous
1916

The Great War Victoria Cross
Heroes
Issued by Gallaher Ltd. 1915

Victoria Cross Heroes
Issued by Cohen Weenen & Co.
1916

Three examples of cards featuring CSM Barter are shown, the first of which was issued by both Thompson & Porteous and Alex Ferguson, the latter being a confectionery firm. The illustration from the set of The Great War Victoria Cross Heroes by Gallaher was one of a series of 200. Cohen Weneen issued their set as one of 50 cards with the maker's name and one of 25, anonymously.

The Great War Victoria Cross
Heroes
Issued by Gallaher Ltd. 1916

Corporal Joseph J. Davies was born in Tipton, Staffordshire, 1899. Initially he became a colliery worker, but enlisted into the 1st Battalion, Royal Welsh Fusiliers in 1909. He then served in Egypt and India, and after he returned to Europe with his battalion in 1914, he was wounded at Ypres in 1915. However, he won his Victoria Cross while serving with the 10th Battalion at Delville Wood on the 20th July 1916. Prior to the attack on the enemy, Corporal Davies and eight men had become separated from the rest of the company. When the enemy delivered a counterattack, the party was completely surrounded, but Corporal Davies got his men into a shell hole, and by throwing bombs and opening rapid fire, he succeeded in routing the attackers and even following and bayoneting them in their retreat. The King presented him with his medal at Buckingham Palace on the 7th October. As he had been badly wounded at Delville Wood, the King had to pin the medal on his sling. He was later promoted to Sergeant and left the Army in December 1918. During the Second World War he served as a Regimental Sergeant-Major with the Poole Cadet Force. He died in 1976.

The Great War Victoria Cross
Heroes
Issued by Gallaher Ltd. 1917

Private Albert Hill, also of the 10th Battalion, was born in Manchester in 1895, one of ten children. He enlisted on the 3rd August 1914 and served in France and Flanders, before winning his Victoria Cross on the 20th July 1916 at Delville Wood. When his battalion was under very heavy fire, Private Hill dashed forward when the order to charge was given and bayoneted two of the enemy. Later, finding himself cut off and almost surrounded by some 20 of the enemy, he attacked them with bombs, killing and wounding many and scattering the rest. He then joined a sergeant of his company and helped him find his way back to their lines, where he heard that his company commander and a scout were wounded. He helped to bring in the wounded officer, and finally captured and brought in two prisoners. He received his medal from the King at Buckingham Palace on November 18th. After the war he emigrated to the United States and became a construction worker. He died at Pawtucket, Rhode Island, in March 1971.

During the First World War four other soldiers won the VC. They were Corporal J.L. Davies, Corporal J. Collins, Lance-Corporal H. Weale and Lance-Sergeant W. Waring.

BOXERS

As with most regiments of the British Army, The Royal Welch Fusiliers had a good boxing team and produced a number of champion boxers, three of which are illustrated cigarette cards.

The first is of Sergeant Basham who was born in Newport, South Wales. He was 5ft 8.5ins in height, weighed 10 stone 7lbs and was the holder of the Welterweight Championship and Lonsdale Belt. He was a very successful boxer from about 1910 and when the cigarette card was produced had only been defeated three times in his career. The example is from a set of 125 cards that was issued by Cope Bros. & Co., a Liverpool based tobacco manufacturer which was founded in 1842.

Next are two examples from the set titled British Army Boxers Series, consisting of 44 subjects. It was issued by Wills (Overseas) with their Scissors cigarettes to British overseas garrisons, mainly India, just before the First World War. The set was very popular and it is unfortunate that it was never issued in the UK.

Corporal Walters, 2nd Battalion Royal Welsh Fusiliers, was born in 1886 and 5ft. 6ins. in height. He was the Bantamweight Champion from India and Burma in 1909.

The final card is of Drummer G. Osborne, also of the 2nd Battalion Royal Welsh Fusiliers, who was born in 1892. He was 5ft. 6ins. in height and weighed 9 stone. He was the Featherweight Champion of the Indian Army from 1911-12 and winner of the King's Gold Medal, Coronation, Durbar from 1911-12

Sergeant Basham

Boxers
Issued by Cope Bros & Co.
1915

Drummer G. Osborne

British Army Boxer Series
Issued by Wills (Overseas)
1913

Corporal Walters

Three interesting personalities that have been associated with the Regiment are shown, the first being of Sir Stapleton Cotton. He only spent a short time with the Regiment becoming an officer in it at 17 years of age. By the time he was 21 he had left to be the Commanding Officer of the 25th Light Dragoons. He was to later become one of Wellington's senior generals in the Peninsula Campaign.

Dandies
Issued by John Player & Sons 1932

Sergeant Luke O'Conner is shown winning his Victoria Cross at the battle of the Alma in the Crimean War. Despite being wounded he carried the Queen's Colour for most of the battle. He was commissioned in the field and later became a Major-General and Colonel of the Regiment.

Colonel R.B. Mainwaring was commissioned in 1871, serving with the 2nd Battalion in the Ashanti Campaign and later with the 1st Battalion. During the Boer War he served on the Staff as AAG and later took part in the advance in Kimberley.

Soldiers of the Queen
Issued by Adkin & Sons 1900

Heroic Deeds
Issued by Wills (Scissors) 1913

The South African Series
Issued by Gallaher Ltd. 1901

REGIMENTAL COLOURS

On this page we see the full colour splendour of the Regimental Colours, as illustrated by John Player & Sons and Gallaher. Unfortunately they are all inaccurate to a greater or lesser extent. The 1903 issue from the John Player set of Badges & Flags of British Regiments is reasonably accurate, although the arrangement of the Battle Honours at the bottom is incorrect and it should have had a Q.V. Crown, not an Imperial one. It was presented to the 1st Battalion in 1880 and retained until 1954. The 2nd Battalion received their Colours in 1859, also replaced in 1954 by H.M The Queen. As such they were both of the pre-1881 style with a Union Flag in the top corner. If they had received new colours after that date then the Regimental Colour would indeed have been similar to the Gallaher illustration. Nevertheless they are all well painted.

Military Series
Issued by John Player & Sons
1900

Regimental Standards & Colours
Issued by Gallaher Ltd.
1899

1903 issue

1903 issue

1904 issue

Badges & Flags of British Regiments issued by John Player & Sons

Further examples of Regimental Colours are shown, two of which represent territorial battalions. In 1908 James Taddy & Co., a tobacco manufacturer based in the East End of London, produced an exceptionally fine set of Territorial Regiments. Illustrated is an example of what the Regimental Colour would have looked like for one of the territorial battalions, after it had presented with new colours after 1908, the only error being that the battalion number had been omitted from the top left hand corner. Before that date the 4th (Denbighshire), 5th (Flintshire) and 6th (Carnarvonshire and Anglesey) Battalions were volunteer battalions of the Regiment.

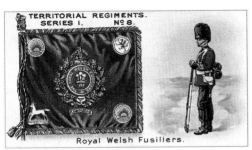

Territorial Regiments
Issued by James Taddy & Co. 1908

Below is another example of a similar Colour, this time of the 7th Battalion. However, the title of 7th (Merionethshire and Montgomeryshire) Battalion was not assumed until 1937. From 1897 until 1908 it was the 5th Volunteer Battalion of the South Wales Borderers, when it became the 7th Battalion, later 7th (Montgomery) Battalion, of The Royal Welsh Fusiliers. At the same time the company based at Aberystwyth University was transferred to the Officers Training Corps. Apart from this title, the illustration is correct. Both examples show the Battle Honour of South Africa 1900-01, won when contingents fought in the Boer War. It was not until 1919 that the Territorial battalions were permitted to bear the other Honours of the Regiment. The final illustration is of a silk card that was issued by Godfrey Phillips in 1918. As described in the previous page, this example is incorrect, as it shows what the Regimental Colour would have looked like if new Colours had indeed been presented to the 2nd Battalion between 1881-1901.

Regimental Colours & Cap Badges - Territorials
Issued by John Player & Sons 1910

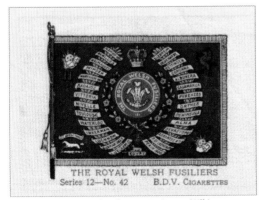

Regimental Colours – Series 12 (Silk)
Issued by Godfrey Phillips Ltd. 1918

REGIMENTAL MASCOTS

The Royal Welsh Fusiliers have had the privilege of having a Regimental Mascot of a Goat for centuries, although no record exists of the origin of the custom. However the first Royal Goat was presented to the Regiment by HM Queen Victoria in 1844 and since then the regular battalions and most of the territorial ones have had a goat presented to them by the Sovereign. Certainly a Goat was present when the Regiment fought at Bunker Hill in 1775 during the American Revolution. The example by Hustler Soap illustrates one of the earlier goats and the uniform of a grenadier company soldier of the period. Two other examples are shown, one being a modern issue by Dandy Gum, and the other by BAT. The latter was also issued by Wills (Scissors) in 1911, one of a set of 33. The illustration by Dandy Gum shows a soldier in Number One dress.

Our Modern Army
Issued by Dandy Gum 1958

Regimental Nicknames
Issued by Hustler Soap 1924

Regimental Mascots
Issued by British American Tobacco Company 1911

Regimental Nicknames
Issued by Hustler Soap 1924

THE SOUTH WALES BORDERERS

On this page are illustrated four examples of different cards featuring the Regimental Colours. The first represents the Queen's Colour of the 1st Battalion, which was recovered from the bottom of Buffalo River in South Africa during the Zulu War. In recognition of the courage shown by the Regiment at Isandhlwana and by Lieutenants Melvill and Coghill who tried to save the Queen's Colour, HM Queen Victoria placed a wreath of Immortelles on the staff of the rescued Colour in 1880. The Regimental Colour had been left at Helpmakaar and is shown in the second example. It was presented to the 1st Battalion in 1866, then the 24th Regiment of Foot, later The 24th (2nd Warwickshire) Regiment of Foot. The next two illustrations are both incorrect and do not represent any Colour carried by either battalion. Whereas the facing colour of the Regiment changed from Grass Green to white in 1881, reverting back to grass green in

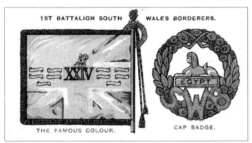

Regimental Standards & Cap Badges
Issued by John Player & Sons 1930

1905, neither battalion was presented with new Colours during this period. As the 2nd Battalion lost both Colours during the Zulu War, they received new ones in 1880. If the 1st Battalion had received new ones between 1881-99, then the illustration by Gallaher would have been correct. However, they did not receive new ones until 1933.

Badges & Flags of British Regts.
Issued by John Player & Sons
1903

Regimental Colours & Standards
Issued by Gallaher Ltd.
1899

Badges & Flags of British Regts.
Issued by John Player & Sons
1904

In 1916 Stephen Mitchell & Son, a Glasgow based tobacco manufacturer and branch of Imperial Tobacco, issued a very attractive set of Army Ribbons & Buttons. Indeed, it is the only set to contain army buttons. As can be seen, it lists the Battle Honours on the reverse that were won by the Regiment before the start of the First World War. The other cards are further examples from the extremely interesting and collectable set of Regimental Pets. It is known that the Regiment had at least two such animals, although unlike the Royal Welch Fusiliers, these were pets and not Regimental Mascots. The first example is of 'Cheeky', a wire-haired terrier, who was the Regimental Dog of the 24th Foot for many years. The other illustration is one of a pair of wildebeeste that were brought back from South Africa by the 2nd Battalion in 1903, after the service in the Boer War. Both of the examples were from a set of 33 Regimental Pets that was issued by Wills (Overseas) with their Scissors cigarettes in 1911. B.A.T. also issued the same set in various other countries, although neither did so after in the United Kingdom.

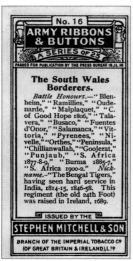

Army Ribbons & Buttons
Issued by Stephen Mitchell & Son 1916

Regimental Pets
Issued by Wills (Scissors) 1911

In 1927 Stephen Mitchell issued two interesting sets of Clan Tartans, the first of 50 cards and the second, as illustrated, of 25. It shows General Sir David Baird, GCB, KC, who was Colonel of the Regiment from 1807 until his death in 1829. Below are three examples from the Boer War Series by F. & J. Smith, another Imperial Tobacco company. Each of the generals illustrated served with the Regiment and are further described on pages 36-39. Finally is an example from Types of the British Army, issued in 1898.

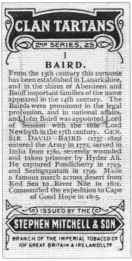

Clan Tartans – 2nd Series
Issued by Stephen Mitchell & Son 1927

Types of the British Army
Issued by Gallaher Ltd. 1898

MAJOR-GEN.
SIR F. CARRINGTON

MAJ.-GEN. CLEMENTS

MAJOR-GEN.
SIR W. PENN SYMONS

Boer War Series (Coloured)
Issued by F. & J. Smith 1901

The History of the V.C.
Issued by John Player & Sons 1980
(Doncella Cigars)

There can be doubt that the bravery of Lieutenants Teignmouth Melvill and Nevill Coghill in trying to save the Queen's Colour at the battle of Isandhlwana is one of the best known deeds to win the Victoria Cross. On the 22nd January 1879, an estimated 20,000 Zulu warriors overran the British camp and killed over 1300 men. As they took no prisoners, and when it became clear that all was clearly lost, the two Lieutenants were ordered to take the Queen's Colour to safety. They reached the Buffalo River, six miles away, when the Zulus caught up with them. Melvill was unhorsed and the Colour carried downstream in the fast running river. Despite his knee injury Coghill, had reached the other bank, but on seeing Melvill in difficulties, returned to assist him, also losing his horse in the process. Both officers then reached the Natal bank and sheltered, but became surrounded. They fought to the last, and when later found, there was a ring of dead Zulus round them. They were both awarded the Victoria Cross for their gallant action.

Victoria Cross
Issued by John Player & Sons
1914

Heroic Deeds
Issued by Wills (Scissors)
1913

Lieutenant T. Melvill was born in London in 1842, educated at Harrow and commissioned into the 24th (2nd Warwickshire) Regiment of Foot in 1865. He became Adjutant in 1875 and entered the Staff College in 1878. However, with the start of the Zulu War he asked to return to his Regiment.

Lieutenant N. Coghill was born in Dublin in 1852 and was also commissioned into the 1st Battalion. When the war broke out he also asked to rejoin his Regiment.

THE ROYAL REGIMENT OF WALES
(24th/41st Foot)

The Royal Regiment of Wales (24th/41st Foot) was formed on 11th June 1969, with the amalgamation of The South Wales Borderers and The Welch Regiment, bringing together two distinguished regiments, whose history goes back three hundred years.

HISTORY OF THE SOUTH WALES BORDERERS

The Regiment has the unique distinction of being an English regiment until 1881, when it became The South Wales Borderers. However, many of its men had been recruited from the Welsh border counties during the late 18th Century, with its Depot established at Brecon in 1873. It was raised by Sir Edward Dering in March 1689, and by August that year, it was in Ireland taking part in the campaign which eventually led to the fall of Limerick. It returned in 1692. It was then known by the names of the different Colonels until 1751, when it was titled The 24th Regiment of Foot. In 1701 Seymour's Regiment, as it was known, sailed for the continent and took part in the War of Spanish Succession. It then served throughout the war and fought in many of Marlborough's battles, such as Blenheim, Ramillies, Oudenarde and Malplaquet. Incidentally the Duke of Marlborough was Colonel of the Regiment from 1702-04. It took part in the Vigo Expedition in 1719, followed by a period of relative inactivity until 1740, when it went to South America. It served in Carthagena and Cuba, and by November 1741, it only had 219 men out of the 1,000 who left England. It then went to Jamaica and returned to England the following year. In 1751 it went to Minorca, and during the Seven Years' War, together with The Royal Welch Fusiliers and two other regiments, it unsuccessfully defended the island against superior forces. A 2nd Battalion was formed in 1756, which became the 69th Foot in 1758, later the 2nd Battalion The Welsh Regiment in 1881. Both battalions were at St. Malo in 1758 and the 1st Battalion served in Germany from 1760-62. In 1776, the Regiment was one of the first to sail for Canada in the American War of Independence. It then served under Burgoyne until his surrender. In 1782 it was re-titled The 24th (2nd Warwickshire) Regiment of Foot.

Following service again in North America from 1789, it returned home in 1800, and the following year, took part in the Expedition to Egypt and the capture of Alexandria. For this action the Regiment was awarded the Sphinx, superscribed 'Egypt'. In 1804 a 2nd Battalion was raised and joined Sir Arthur Wellesley's Army in Portugal in 1809. It then took part in the different battles in Spain, winning nine Honours, the most significant of which was Talavera, where the Battalion suffered heavy casualties holding the line against a fierce attack. It was disbanded in 1814. Meanwhile the 1st Battalion went to the Cape of Good Hope in 1806 and later to India in 1810. The next major action for the Regiment was during the 2nd Sikh War in 1848-49, where it fought at Sadoolapore, Chillianwallah and Goojerat. It then served on the North West Frontier from 1855-56. During the Indian Mutiny it was stationed in the Punjab, suffering many casualties.

It is for their service the Zulu War of 1879 that the Regiment will probably be best remembered. Both battalions were engaged, with five companies of the 1st and one of the 2nd camped at Iswandhlwana when they were attacked, defeated and all killed by a force of 20,000 Zulus. As has already been mentioned, two officers gained the Victoria Cross for trying to save the Queen's Colour. At the same time, B Company of the 2nd Battalion was attacked by a force of 4,000 Zulus at Rorke's Drift, about ten miles away. Despite being heavily outnumbered the small force drove off the attackers, with Lieutenant Bromhead and six other members of the Regiment being awarded the Victoria Cross. In 1881 the Regiment became the South Wales Borderers. Unfortunately the grass green facings were replaced with white, but these were restored in 1905. With the start of the Boer War in 1900, the 2nd Battalion was once again sent back to South Africa, forming part of the 15th Brigade. Although they did not see much of the fighting, about 200 men formed the main part of the post at Modderfontein, when a much superior force attacked it in January 1901. They fought well before being forced to surrender, losing 10 men killed and nine wounded. Lord Kitchener mentioned eight men for exceptional gallantry, including a DCM for Lance-Corporal H. Blair. Meanwhile the 1st Battalion was in India and returned to England in December 1910.

At the start of the First World War the 1st Battalion went to France as part of the 1st Division and took part in the Retreat from Mons. Meanwhile, the 2nd Battalion was in China as part of the international force. Indeed, they were the only British unit to gain the Battle Honour "Tsingtao", for their part in the capture of the German Treaty port. It would be impossible to detail the war service of the Regiment, but during the First World War they raised 18 battalions, gained 74 Battle Honours and were awarded six Victoria Crosses. However, they also lost 5,777 men. After the end of hostilities both regular battalions formed part of the Army of Occupation of Germany. Between the wars both battalions found themselves posted to various parts of the Empire, including Egypt, Palestine, Hong Kong, India, Malta and Ireland. Once again with the start of the Second World War the Regiment was expanded and fought in various theatres, including North West Europe and Burma. Indeed the 2nd Battalion was the only Welsh Regiment to land on the beaches of Normandy

After the war the Regiment, now a single battalion unit, was posted to Palestine, followed by Malaya and later Aden. It is interesting to note that while serving in Hong Kong in 1966 they were relieved by their future partners, The Welch Regiment.

These pictures are only issued with the
CRAYOL VIRGINIA
and
KARAM TURKISH Cigarettes.

Soldiers & Their Uniforms
Issued by Major Drapkin & Co. 1914

PERSONALITES

John Churchill, 1st Duke of Marlborough, KG, was one of the most distinguished soldiers of the British Army. His association with the Regiment started on the 12th February 1702 when he was appointed Colonel, a position he held until 1704. Illustrated is a small selection of cards on which he is featured.

Builders of the British Army
Issued by J.A. Pattreiouex 1929

Devon Worthies
Issued by James Pascall 1927

Builders of the Empire
Issued by J. Wix & Sons Ltd. 1937

Miniatures – No Border
Issued by R.J. Lea Ltd. 1912

Leaders of Men
Issued by Ogdens Ltd. 1924

Miniatures – Gold Border
Issued by R.J. Lea Ltd. 1912

Major-General R.A.P. Clements was the son of Reverend J. Clements, the sub-Dean of Lincoln Cathedral. He was educated at Rossall and commissioned into the Regiment in 1874, promoted Captain 1880, Major 1886, Lieutenant-Colonel 1887 and Colonel 1896. He served in the Kaffir War 1877-78, the Zulu War 1879 and the Burmese Expedition 1885-89, where he won the DSO. In the Boer War he commanded the 12th Brigade. He is shown on a number of cards of the Boer War period.

The South African Series
Issued by Gallaher Ltd.
1901

Boer War & Actresses – Base F
Issued by Ogdens (Guinea Gold)
1901

General Interest Series B
Issued by Ogdens (Tabs)
1901

Celebrities – Coloured
Issued by Cohen Weenen
1901

Transvaal Series
Issued by W.D. & H.O. Wills
1901

Boer War – Series A
Issued by American Tobacco Co.
1901

Major-General Sir William P. Symons, KCB, was commissioned into the Regiment in 1863, promoted Lieutenant in 1866, Captain 1878, Major 1881, Lieutenant-Colonel 1886 and Colonel 1887. He served in the Kaffir War of 1877-78, the Zulu campaign of 1879 and in the Burmese Expedition in 1885-89 as Deputy Assistant Adjutant and Quartermaster General, in which he also organised the Mounted Infantry. He was then given command of the China Field Force with the rank of Brigadier-General, in which he was several times mentioned in despatches. From 1889-90 he commanded the Burma Column in the Chin-Lushai Expedition and later commanded a brigade of the Waziristan Field Force from 1894-95, for which he received the thanks of the Government of India. At the start of the Boer War he was in command in Natal. Unfortunately he was severely wounded at the battle of Glencoe in October 1899 and died a few days later.

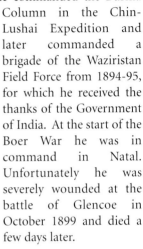

The South African Series Issued by Gallaher Ltd. 1901	Boer War & General – Base D Issued by Ogdens (Guinea Gold) 1901

Transvaal War – With Text
Issued by W.D. & H.O. Wills
1901

Celebrities – Coloured
Issued by Cohen Weenen
1901

Transvaal Series – No Text
Issued by W.D. & H.O. Wills
1902

Another distinguished soldier who served with the Regiment was Major-General Sir Frederick Carrington, KCB, KCMG. He was commissioned in 1864 and rose rapidly in rank to become a Lieutenant-Colonel in 1879 and Major-General in 1894. Whilst serving in South Africa in the 1870's he raised and commanded a number of mounted infantry units, including the Frontier Light Horse. He later served in the Boer War.

Celebrities (Coloured)
Issued by Cohen Weenen 1901

The South Africa Series
Issued by Gallaher Ltd. 1901

Celebrities (Coloured)
Issued by Cohen Weenen 1901

Boer War Celebrities
Issued by Drapkin & Millhoff
1901

Soldiers of the Queen
Issued by Adkin & Sons
1900

Transvaal Series
Issued by W.D. & H.O. Wills
1901

The illustrations of General Carrington are from a wide variety of manufacturers, although all were issued about 1901. Of particular interest is the pair of cards from the set of Celebrities by Cohen Weenen. As can be seen they show him in two different poses, one with two and the other four medals. Next is further example from the South African Series by Gallaher. Soldiers of the Queen was issued as a set of both 50 and 60. As can be seen all of the other illustrations are based on the same photograph, although they were all issued by different firms.

The other personality is of the actor and radio celebrity Reginald Purdell. Born in London in 1896, he started his acting career in 1911 playing a child actor in Romeo and Juliet. During the First World War he was an officer in The South Wales Borderers and the RAF. Afterwards he turned to musical comedy and was in 'Damsel in Distress', 'Middle Watch' and 'Orders are Orders'. He appeared in many films, including 'On the Air'. The illustration of him in from the 1935 set of Radio Favourites by John Sinclair, a company based in Newcastle-on-Tyne, owned by Carreras.

Boer War & Miscellaneous
Issued by Ogdens (Guinea Gold) 1900

Radio Favourites	Leading Generals of the War	Guinea Gold Series
Issued by John Sinclair Ltd.	Issued by Ogdens (Tabs)	issued by Godfrey Phillips
1935	1901	1902

In 1994 Richie & Co., a firm of Chartered Accountants based in Cardiff, produced an attractive set of 25 trade cards titled Heroes of the Zulu Wars. Not surprisingly a number of them featured officers of both the 1st and 2nd Battalions of the 24th (2nd Warwickshire) Regiment of Foot, all of whom were killed at Isandlwana in January 1979.

Captain Reginald Younghusband
(1st Battalion)

Lieutenant Francis P. Porteous
(1st Battalion)

Lieutenant George F.J. Hodson
(1st Battalion)

Lieutenant Charles J. Atkinson
(1st Battalion)

Lieutenant Neville J.A. Coghill
(1st Battalion)

Lieutenant Charles D'A. Pope
(2nd Battalion)

Heros of the Zulu Wars
Issued by Richie and Co 1994

VICTORIA CROSS WINNERS

Lieutenant Gonville Bromhead was one of six members of the 2nd Battalion to win the Victoria Cross at the defence of Rorke's Drift during the Zulu War of 1879. He was born in 1844 in France, educated at Newark and commissioned into the Regiment in April 1867. He shared command of the garrison and won his medal for conspicuous gallantry in the engagement. He was also promoted to Captain and given the Brevet of Major. He later fought in the Burmese Expeditions of 1885 and 1887-89 and died in Lucknow, India in 1891.

Victoria Cross Heroes
Issued by Ogdens Ltd. 1901

Private Alfred Henry Hook was born at Churcham, Gloucester, and served for five years in the Monmouthshire Militia before joining the Regiment. He served throughout the Kaffir War of 1877-78 and won his Victoria Cross for his part in defending the hospital wing of the mission station and helping the wounded to be evacuated. Lord Wolseley presented him with his medal on the 3rd August 1879. He later served as a Sergeant in the 1st Volunteer Battalion Royal Fusiliers and became a member of staff of the British Museum. He died in Gloucester in March 1905.

Shown are some examples of cards of the two men, two of which were issued by Ogdens. Of the other two cards, the one by Taddy and Co. is the most valuable.

Victoria Cross Heroes
Issued by James Taddy & Co.
1901

Victoria Cross
Issued by John Player & Sons
1914

Illustrated are examples of cards of another two soldiers who won the Victoria Cross at Rorke's Drift. They are of Privates William and Robert Jones, who, together with Privates Frederick Hitch, William Allen and Alfred Henry Hook, won their medals for defending the hospital wing for over an hour and evacuating the wounded. Private William Jones was born at Evesham in Worcestershire in 1840 and Private Robert Jones at Raglan in Monmouthshire in August 1857. They both enlisted into the 2nd battalion of the Regiment. During the engagement they both defended one of the wards of the hospital until six out of the seven patients had been removed. The seventh was delirious, and although they managed to dress him, they could not persuade him to move. When they later returned to carry him away, they found that he had been stabbed to death. Private William Jones was discharged from the Army Reserve in January 1888 and died at Ardwick in Lancashire in 1913. Robert Jones died at Madley in Hereford in September 1898.

On this and the previous page, three of the illustrations are from the Ogdens set of Victoria Cross Heroes. It was issued as one of 50 cards, and although they are not of the same quality as the two by James Taddy & Co., they are still very collectable. Taddy issued a total of 125 cards of Victoria Cross winners between 1901 and 1904. The other two cards were issued by John Player & Sons, a Nottingham branch of Imperial Tobacco.

Victoria Cross Heroes
Issued by James Taddy & Co.
1901

Victoria Cross Heroes
Issued by Ogdens Ltd.
1901

The History of the V.C.
Issued by John Player & Sons (Doncella Cigars) 1980

The Great War Victoria Cross Heroes
Issued by Gallaher Ltd. 1915-18

Of the six members of the Regiment to be awarded the Victoria Cross during the First World War, two are illustrated on cigarette cards.

The first is of Lieutenant (Temporary Captain) Angus Buchanan of the 4th Battalion, who won his award on the 5th April 1916 at Falauyah Lines in Mesopotamia. During an attack, when another officer was lying in the open severely wounded about 150 yards from cover, two men went out to his assistance with one of them being hit at once. On seeing this Captain Buchanan immediately went out, and with the assistance of the other soldier, carried the first casualty to cover under machine-gun fire. He then led and brought back the other wounded man, again under heavy fire. During the war he also won the Military Cross and the Order of St. Vladimir - 4th Class with Swords of Russia. He died in Gloucester in 1944.

The other card is of Private James Henry Fynn, also of the 4th Battalion, who won his Victoria Cross on the 9th April 1916 at Sanna-i-Yat in Mesopotamia. He was one of a small party, which was dug in, in front of the British lines, about 300 yards from the enemy's trenches. He went out and bandaged a number of wounded men under heavy fire, making several journeys in order to do so. Being unable to get a stretcher, he carried back a badly wounded man to safety. He was killed in March and is commemorated on the Basra War Memorial in Iraq and The Guildhall in Bodmin, Cornwall.

In total 21 members of the Regiment have been awarded the Victoria Cross, five of them in 1867, at Little Andaman in the Bay of Bengal, all of the 2nd Battalion. They were Assistant Surgeon Campbell Mellis Douglas and Privates David Bell, James Cooper, William Griffiths and Thomas Murphy. Lieutenant, The Lord Edric Frederick Gifford, also of the 2nd Battalion, won his at Becquah in the Ashanti in 1874 and nine others during the Zulu War of 1879. In addition to the eight already mentioned, Lieutenant Edward Stevenson Browne of the 1st Battalion won his at Holobane Mountain. The four other recipients of the First World War were Sergeant Albert White, 2nd Battalion, Sergeant Ivor Rees, 11th Battalion, Company Sergeant-Major John Henry Williams, 10th Battalion, and Lieutenant-Colonel Dudley Graham Johnson, whilst attached to the 2nd Battalion The Royal Sussex Regiment.

All of these illustrations are from one of the most popular sets that was issued, initially by John Player & Sons in 1909, but later by several other branches of Imperial Tobacco. Below is a selection of examples of the very many different backs, together with the painting of a Private in 1760 at about the time of the conquest of Canada. The John Player overseas set had a grey back with the set consisting of 50 subjects. The set can also be found with four other different backs, including Vice Regal and Havelock brands.

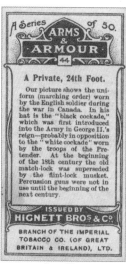

Issued by
Hignett Bros. & Co. 1924

Issued by
John Player (Overseas) 1926

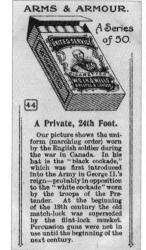

Issued by
Wills (United Service) 1910

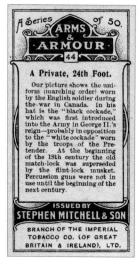

Issued by
Stephen Mitchell & Son 1916

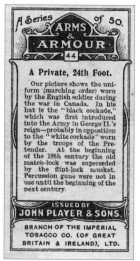

Issued by
John Player & Sons 1909

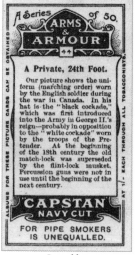

Issued by
Wills (Australia) 1910

Here are shown a number of examples of cards of Regimental badges, three of which are silk issues. The first is from the 1924-25 set of 150 Army, Corps & Divisional Sign that was issued by John Player & Sons. This particular card illustrates three examples of the battalion signs used by the Regiment during the First War. Next is another example from the 1923 set of paper backed silk Regimental Badges that was issued by R.J. Lea, a firm based in Stockport near Manchester. The large illustration is from one of a number of different silk sets of Regimental Badges that was issued by B. Murratti Sons & Co. Ltd., another firm founded in Manchester. It was later incorporated into the UK. Tobacco Company in London. John Sinclair also issued a similar set in 1915. Finally is an example from one of a number of the different sets on Crests & Badges that was issued by Phillips.

Army, Corps & Divisional Signs
Issued by John Player 1925

Regimental Crests & Badges (Silk)
Issued by R.J. Lea 1923

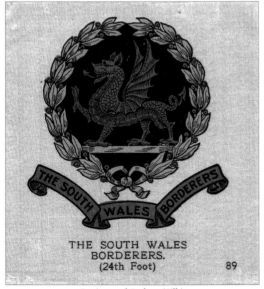

Regimental Badges (Silk)
Issued by B. Murratti Sons & Co. Ltd. 1915

Crests & Badges of the British Army
Issued by Godfrey Phillips Ltd. 1914

Further examples of Regimental badges are shown, with two of the illustrations being from the set of Army Crests & Mottoes that was issued by Ogdens of Liverpool in 1902. It consisted of 192 subjects. Also shown is another silk issue, this time by E. & W. Anstie. The example from the set of British Uniforms of the 19th Century shows a soldier at the time of the Zulu War, although unfortunately the tunic is incorrect. The cuffs and collar should be green, as they did not change to white until 1881. ABC Cinemas shows an officer about 1750 and the other a Drummer in South Africa in 1900.

Army Crests & Mottoes
Issued by Ogdens Ltd. 1902

Regimental Badges (Silk)
Issued by E.W. Anstie 1915

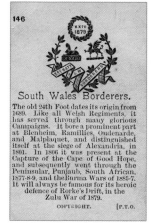

Army Crests & Mottoes
Issued by Ogdens Ltd. 1902

British Uniforms of the 19th C.
Issued by Mills Filtertips 1957

British Soldiers
Issued by ABC Cinemas 1949

Military
Issued by John Brindley 1987

HISTORY OF THE MONMOUTHSHIRE REGIMENT

G.P. Territorial Badges (Silk)
Issued by Godfrey Phillips Ltd. 1913

The Monmouthshire Regiment was formed in 1908 from volunteer battalions affiliated to the South Wales Borderers. The 1st (Rifle) Battalion was originally formed in 1860 from the 1st, 3rd, 4th, 10th and 11th Corps of Monmouthshire Rifle Volunteers and consolidated as the 1st Corps in 1880. It later became the 2nd Volunteer Battalion, South Wales Borderers and received the Honour 'South Africa 1900-02' for services in the Boer War. In February 1915 the 1/1st Battalion went to France and later became the pioneer battalion of 46th Division, while a duplicate battalion, the 2/1st, remained in the UK and was disbanded in 1918. The 3/1st became the 1st (Reserve) Battalion and later also disbanded. In 1930 the Battalion was converted, and the following year, became 68th Searchlight Regiment, Royal Artillery.

The 2nd Battalion was formed in 1859 as the 2nd Monmouthshire Rifle Volunteer Corps and redesignated as the 3rd Volunteer Battalion, South Wales Borderers in 1885. It also contributed large numbers for service in South Africa. In 1914-18 the 1/2nd Battalion served in France as pioneers, while the 2/2nd and 3/2nd remained in the UK. During the Second World War the Battalion fought in NW Europe as part of 53rd Infantry Division. In 1947 it was amalgamated with the 4th Battalion and is currently part of the 3rd (Volunteer) Battalion, The Royal Regiment of Wales.

The 3rd (Brecknockshire and Monmouthshire) Battalion was formed in 1880 as the 3rd Monmouthshire Rifle Volunteer Corps from several corps that had previously constituted the 2nd Admin Battalion of Monmouthshire Rifle Volunteers. It became the 4th Volunteer Battalion, South Wales Borderers in 1885 and also provided a number of volunteers for service in South Africa. It became the 3rd Battalion, Monmouthshire Regiment in 1908 and during the First World War it served as a pioneer battalion in 49th Division. In 1922 it amalgamated with the Brecknockshire Battalion, South Wales Borderers to form the 3rd (Brecknockshire and Monmouthshire) Battalion, Monmouthshire Regiment. In 1939 the Battalion was split by county, with the Monmouthshire section serving in NW Europe in 1944-45, while the Brecknockshire Battalion remained in the UK. In 1947 both the Monmouth and Brecknock Battalions were transferred to the Royal Artillery as 637 and 638 LAA Regiments.

The 4th Battalion was formed in 1916 and disbanded in 1919. A new 4th Battalion was formed in 1939, which served in the UK and amalgamated with the 2nd Battalion in 1947.

THE WELCH REGIMENT

Illustrated are a number of cards showing the Regimental Pets of both the 1st and 2nd Battalions, together with examples of both the Regimental badge and buttons. It is believed that the 1st Battalion of the Regiment, then the 41st Foot, first adopted the Goat Mascot during the Crimean War, although the first official one was about 1860. He was presented by HM. Queen Victoria and known as Billy. However, the three illustrations are of much later animals. In fact the 69th Foot did not have such a Mascot until they became the 2nd Battalion of the Welsh Regiment in 1881. However, each was named Taffy, not Billy, with Taffy IV being the one in service in 1911. Nevertheless, all three examples are very attractive and collectable, with the two by Wills being issued in India with their Scissors cigarettes and the one by Gallaher with various tobacco brands in the UK. The other two cards show the Regiments Badge, button and ribbon.

Army Ribbons & Buttons
Issued by S. Mitchell & Son
1916

Types of the British Army
Issued by Gallaher Ltd.
1898

Regimental Pets
Issued by Wills (Scissors) 1911

Army Badges
Issued by Gallaher Ltd. 1939

Regimental Pets
Issued by Wills (Scissors) 191

HISTORY OF THE WELCH REGIMENT

The 1st Battalion of the Regiment, the 41st Foot, was raised in 1719 as a regiment of Invalids from Royal Hospital Chelsea pensioners for garrison duty at home. They were originally known as Colonel Edmund Fielding's Regiment of Invalids and redesignated The 41st Regiment of Foot (or Invalids) in 1751. However, in 1787 it ceased to be an invalid regiment and became an infantry regiment of the line, with the pensioners being discharged. After a period of extensive recruitment, in which the later Duke of Wellington briefly served with it, the Regiment went to the West Indies in 1793 and served at the capture of Martinique, St. Lucia and Guadeloupe. In 1796, as a result of its numbers being greatly reduced, the Privates were transferred to the 17th Foot and the Officers and NCOs returned to the UK. Once it had been brought up to strength again, it went to Canada in 1799 and was actively engaged in the Anglo-American War of 1812. The Regiment returned home in 1815 and then formed part of the Army of Occupation of France. It then went to India in 1822 and took part in the 1st Burma War of 1824-26, followed years of garrison duty. In 1831 it was re-titled The 41st or the Welch Regiment of Infantry, later 41st (Welch) Regiment in 1838. Four years later, shortly before it returned to Wales, it took part in the invasion of Afghanistan and gained three further Battle Honours. It served in the Crimea from 1854-56 and fought at Alma, Inkerman and Sevastopol, gaining two Victoria Crosses. Almost immediately after its return to England, it was sent to the West Indies again, where it stayed until 1860. There then followed periods of service in Ireland, India, Aden, Natal and Gibraltar. In 1881 the Regiment amalgamated with The 69th (South Lincolnshire) Regiment of Foot to form The Welsh Regiment, with a Depot at Cardiff.

Originally raised as the 2nd Battalion of the 24th Foot, the 69th Foot became a regiment in its own right in 1758, being retitled The 69th (South Lincolnshire) Regiment of Foot in 1782. Between 1758 and 1800 the Regiment spent a great deal of service on board the Fleet acting as marines and taking part in many battles, including The Glorious First of June and St. Vincent. Indeed it is the only British Regiment to have two Naval Battle Honours, namely a Naval Crown superscribed 12th April 1782, for the battle of the Saints, and St. Vincent for its service at the battle in 1797. A Second Battalion was raised during the Napoleonic War and fought at Quatre Bra and Waterloo, but disbanded in 1816, with its remaining personnel absorbed by the 1st Battalion, which was then in India. Here it fought in many campaigns, including Travancore in 1809, Bourbon and Mauritius 1810, Java 1811 and the Mahratta War 1817-20, returning home in 1826. The Regiment then served in England from 1826-31, followed by various periods of overseas and home service, including Nova Scotia, Malta, West Indies, Burma and India. In 1867 it went to Canada and service on the US/Canadian border against Fenian raids. Later, they went to Bermuda and Gibraltar, before returning to England and the amalgamation of 1881, when it became the 2nd Battalion of The Welsh Regiment.

The 1st Battalion then saw service in Natal, Egypt and later in the Boer War, in which they were supported by volunteer companies drawn from the four Volunteer Battalions.

Meanwhile the 2nd Battalion went to India in 1892, where it spent almost fourteen years, before spending four years in garrison duty in South Africa from 1906-10. It was then posted to Wales until the start of the First World War. The 1st Battalion had already returned home in 1904, before being sent to Egypt in 1909 and later to India, although with the start of the First World War it was ordered back to the UK. The regiment then expanded to 34 battalions, of which 19 served overseas. The 1st Battalion returned from India in December 1914 and landed in France as part of 28th Division in January 1915. However, it sailed from Marseilles for Salonika, via Egypt in November and then served in the Middle East. The 2nd Battalion was part of 1st Division and one of the first to go to France as part of the British Expeditionary Force. It spent the entire war in France and Flanders. It would be impossible to list the war service of all of the active service battalions, but in total they gained over 70 Battle Honours and won three Victoria Crosses. However, they also suffered losses of 7,679 officers, NCOs and men killed. Illustrated are two examples of the signs of the Divisions in which the different battalions served. After the war the Regiment was reduced to its peacetime strength of two regular battalions, with the 1st Battalion being sent to India and the 2nd Battalion seeing service during the troubles in Ireland. At the start of the Second World War the Regiment was again expanded, with its various battalions serving in the Western Desert, Crete, Italy, Burma and NW Europe. In total they won a further 22 Battle Honours and lost 1,000 Officers and Men killed. In line with other infantry regiments, The Welch Regiment was reduced to a single battalion in 1948 and later served in the Korean War. It then served in various postings, including Germany, Cyprus, Libya and Hong Kong, before the amalgamation of 1969.

5th Battalion Welsh Regiment.

Regimental Colours & Cap Badges
Issued by John Player & Sons 1910

(Red)   (Natural Colours)

(Army, Corps & Divisional Signs issued by John Player & Sons 1924-25

REGIMENTAL COLOURS

On this page are illustrated a number of examples of cards featuring the Regimental Colours of the Welch Regiment, although once again there are a few minor errors. The first is a silk issue that was produced by B. Morris & Son Ltd., a London based manufacturer. It appears to be correct and represents the Regimental Colour Lord Kitchener presented that to the Regiment in 1910, and which remained in use until 1948. The 1904 issue from the John Player & Sons set of Badges & Flags of British Regiments

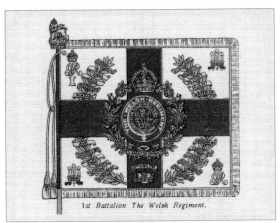

1st Battalion The Welsh Regiment.

Regimental Colours (Silk)
Issued by M. Morris & Sons Ltd. 1916

illustrates the previous Colour that was in use from 1862 until 1910. It was of the pre-1881 style with a small Union Flag in the top corner. On the other hand the 1903 issue shows the Regimental Colour of the 2nd Battalion that was taken into use in 1899. However it should have had a Queen Victorian Crown. The final illustration by Players shows both the Queen's and Regimental Colours of the Regiment.

Military Series
Issued by John Player & Sons
1900

1904 issue

1903 issue

Badges & Flags of British Regiments
Issued by John Player & Sons

The first illustration shows a Private of the 69th (South Lincolnshire) Regiment in 1815, and is one of a set of 50 cards from a set of the History of Army Uniforms, issued by Carreras in 1937. It also shows the green facings worn by the Regiment until 1881, after which they changed to white, on becoming the 2nd Battalion of The Welsh Regiment. The other four examples, three of which are in silk, are all of Regimental Badges from various different firms.

History of Army Uniforms
Issued by Carreras Ltd. 1937

Army Crests & Mottoes
Issued by Ogdens Ltd. 1902

Regimental Badges (Silk)
Issued by E. & W. Anstie
1915

Regimental Badges (Silk)
Issued by John Sinclair Ltd. 1915

Crests & Badges of the British Army
Issued by Godfrey Phillips 1914

Lance-Corporal William Charles Fuller was one of three members of the Regiment, and the first Welshman, to win the Victoria Cross during the First World War. He was born in 1884 at Newbridge, Laugharne, Carmarthenshire and moved to Swansea four years later. He enlisted into the regiment in 1902 and served in South Africa and India. He was recalled in August 1914 at the start of the war. Indeed, it was shortly afterwards on the 14th September, that he won his Victoria Cross near Chivy-sur-Aisne in France. He advanced under very heavy rifle and machine-gun fire to pick up a wounded officer, Captain Mark Haggard, who was mortally wounded, and carried him back to cover. He was promoted to Sergeant, but left the Army in 1915. In 1938 he was presented with the Royal Humane Society Medal for rescuing two boys who had fallen into the sea. He died in 1974.

War Series L
Issued by Murray Sons & Co. Ltd. 1916

Victoria Cross Heroes
Issued by Cohen Weenen 1915

Victoria Coss Heroes
Issued by Wills (Scissors)
1915

V.C. Heroes
Issued by Alex Ferguson
1916

The Great War Victoria Cross
Heroes
Issued by Gallaher Ltd. 1915

The other two members of the Regiment to be awarded the Victoria Cross during the First World War were Second-Lieutenant Edgar Kingthorn Myles of the 8th Battalion and Private Hubert William Lewis of the 11th Battalion.

Lieutenant Myles was born in Wanstead, Essex in 1894 and enlisted into the 9th Battalion Worcestershire Regiment in 1914. He was commissioned in October and transferred into The Welsh Regiment in August 1915, only to be

The Great War Victoria Cross Heroes
Issued by Gallaher Ltd. 1915-18

posted back to the Worcestershire Regiment almost immediately. He was his medal on the 9th April 1916 at Sanna-i-Yat in Mesopotamia by going out alone several times in front of the trenches and, under heavy rifle fire and at great personal risk, helped wounded men lying in the open. On one occasion he carried in a wounded officer to a place of safety under circumstances of great danger. In addition to the Victoria Cross, he was also awarded the Distinguished Service Order and promoted Captain. A keen golfer, he died at Bishopsteignton in Devon in 1977.

Private Lewis was born in Milford Haven in Pembrokeshire in 1896 and enlisted into 11th (Service) Battalion (Cardiff Pals) in September 1914. He won his Victoria Cross on the 22/23 October 1916 at Macukovo, near Seres in Salonika. When on duty during a raid, Private Lewis was twice wounded on reaching the enemy trenches, but refused to be attended to. He was wounded again while searching enemy dugouts and again refused assistance. At this point three of the enemy approached and Private Lewis immediately attacked them single-handed, capturing all three. Later, during the retirement, he went to the assistance of a wounded man and, under heavy shell and rifle fire, brought him back safely, after which he collapsed. He was also awarded the Medaille Militaire of France. During the Second World War he served as a Sergeant in the Milford Haven Home Guard, with one of his three sons being killed with the RAF. He later died at Milford Haven in 1977.

Three other members of the Regiment were awarded the Victoria Cross, but do not appear on any cigarette card. They were Sergeant-Major Ambrose Madden and Captain Hugh Rowlands during the Crimean War and Lieutenant Tasker Watkins of the 1/5th Battalion in France in 1944. In total the Regiment won six such awards.

Here are shown a number of other interesting personalities who were associated with the Regiment. Firstly are two illustrations of Sir Ralph Abercromby, KB, who was the Colonel of the 69th (South Lincolnshire) Regiment of Foot from 1790-92. Next is a portrait of HRH. The Prince of Wales in the uniform an officer of the Regiment. The third personality of General Sir William F. Butler, KCB, who was also commissioned in the 69th. He served with the Regiment in Canada and throughout the Ashanti war of 1873. Promoted Colonel, he was in Egypt in 1882 and with the Nile Expedition of 1884-85. He commanded a brigade in the Egyptian Frontier Field Force from 1885-86 and promoted Major-General 1992. He was later appointed C-in-C in South Africa, although he was recalled for political reasons just before the Boer War.

Famous Scots	Builders of the Empire
Issued by Stephen Mitchell & Son 1933	Issued by J. Wix & Sons Ltd. 1937

Silver Jubilee
Issued by Ardath Tobacco Co.
1935

The South African series
issued by Gallaher Ltd.
1901

The Transvaal Series
Issued by W.D. & H.O. Wills
1901

AUTHOR

David Hunter was born in Glasgow in 1942 and educated at Daniel Stewart's College, Edinburgh. He joined the army in 1964 and served in the Intelligence Corps. After having left the army in 1970, he joined the Sales Force of the cigarette manufacturer John Player & Sons and was based for some time in rural Wales. Having taken early retirement four years ago he now runs a small part-time business buying and selling cigarette cards. He is an active member of the Military Historical Society, having been its Honorary Secretary for a short while. He is also a magistrate on the Nottingham bench.

PRIVATE 24TH (2ND WARWICKSHIRE) FOOT

Caricatures of the British Army
Issued by Victoria Gallery 1994

TITLES PUBLISHED

The Gordon Highlanders
The Worcestershire & Sherwood Foresters Regiment
The Queen's Royal Lancers
The Scots Guards
The Royal Regiment of Fusiliers - Part 1 (5th & 6th Foot)
The Royal Regiment of Fusiliers - Part 2 (7th & 20th Foot)
The Coldstream Guards
Queen's Own Highlanders (Seaforth & Camerons)
The Regiments of Wales